DEC 2002

S0-ARJ-846

3 1524 00365 2536

WITHDRAWN
Woodridge Public Library

Hill, Valerie.
Korea

J
900
Hil

MAY - 5 2003			
OCT 1 4 2003			
MAY 0 6 2004			
AUG 0 6 2007			

WOODRIDGE PUBLIC LIBRARY
3 PLAZA DRIVE
WOODRIDGE, IL 60517-5014
(630) 964-7899

ASK
ABOUT

ASIA

Mason Crest Publishers Inc.
370 Reed Road
Broomall, Pennsylvania 19008
(866) MCP-BOOK (toll free)

Copyright © 2003 by Mason Crest Publishers. All rights reserved. No part of this publication may be reproduced or transmitted in any form or by any means, electronic or mechanical, including photocopying, recording, taping, or any information storage and retrieval system, without permission in writing from the publisher.

First printing

1 2 3 4 5 6 7 8 9 10

Library of Congress Cataloging-in-Publication Data on file at the Library of Congress.

ISBN 1-59084-206-5
ISBN 1-59084-198-0 (series)

Printed in Malaysia.

Adapted from original concept produced by
Vineyard Freepress Pty Ltd., Sydney
Copyright © 1999 Vineyard Freepress Pty Ltd.

Project Editor	Valerie Hill
Text	Valerie Hill
Design	Denny Allnutt
Research	Peter Barker
Copy Editor	Philippa Yelland
Cartography	Ray Sim
Consultant	Young Gil Lim
Cover Design	Vineyard Freepress
Images	Korean National Tourist Organisation, *Seoul* Magazine, Mike Langford, Consulate-General of the Republic of Korea, Korean Overseas Information Service, *Korea Trading Post* Magazine, Chosun Gallery Sydney, Valerie Hill, Peter Barker.

COVER: Masked folk dance, Hahoe Cultural Village.

TITLE PAGE: Folding screen symbolizing royal authority stood behind the throne.

CONTENTS: Cyclist on his way to market in the Andong region.

INTRODUCTION: Villagers of Chunghak-dong say farewell to a relative leaving by bus after the harvest.

Korea

MASON CREST PUBLISHERS

WOODRIDGE PUB. LIB.

CONTENTS

THE LAND

THE NATION

WAR AND DIVISION

MODERN SOUTH KOREA

DAILY LIFE

INTRODUCTION

KOREA is one of the few countries in the world to have continued as one nation with one language since its earliest history. For thousands of years the people of this small peninsula, overshadowed by nearby countries, maintained their unique identity and culture. Now Korea communicates and trades with many countries all over the world, and its people live in a time of great change.

The nation's unity was broken in the 1950s by a bitter war which left North and South divided. This book follows South Korea's astonishing rise from the desolation of war into a vibrant country which has modernized its whole way of life in a very short time. Well-educated, with advanced technology, South Koreans pass on their proud cultural heritage to their children.

THE KOREAN PENINSULA

▲ Herons, found throughout Korea, symbolize purity and peace.

▼ Paddy fields in the southwest.

Extending from the Asian continent, the world's largest land mass, the Korean peninsula is among the smallest of the Asian countries, with a length of about 600 miles (1,000 kilometers). In the north, where Korea shares boundaries with China and Russia, high forested peaks and deep gorges are rich in minerals, especially coal. But there is little arable land, and lakes and rivers freeze over during harsh winters. In the south, the granite mountain ranges extend like a backbone down the east coast, with almost vertical rock faces plunging into the deep East Sea (Sea of Japan). This steep rocky barrier protects Korea from typhoons, *tsunami,* and seaborne enemy invasion. Of the total land area, only 30 percent can be farmed. The fertile, warmer plains of the southwest provide most of the country's food. The shallow West Sea (Yellow Sea) is a safe harbor rich in shellfish. To the east and south are deep-sea fishing grounds.

CLIMATE

Korea is in the temperate zone of the northern hemisphere. Located in the East Asian monsoon belt, it has hot, humid summers and long, dry, cold winters, which are usually more severe in the north, with short but pleasant and colorful autumn and spring seasons.

Say it in KOREAN !
Island *-do* as in Cheju-do
Province *-ju* as in Che-ju
Mountain *-san* as in Halla-san
River *-gang* as in Han-gang

FACT FILE

NORTH KOREA

Official Name: Democratic People's Republic of Korea, founded in 1948

Official Language: Korean

Population: 23,900,000

Capital: Pyongyang (Population: 2,639,000)

Currency: Won ₩

Land Area: 46,490 sq miles (120,410 sq km)

Ethnic Groups: Korean 99.8%; Chinese 0.2%

Religions: Nonreligious 67.9%; Traditional Beliefs 15.6%; Ch'ongdogyo 13.9%; Buddhist 1.7%; Christian 0.9%

Major Physical Features: Highest mountain: Paektusan 9,003 ft (2,744 m); Longest river: Amnokkang 493 miles (790 km)

SOUTH KOREA

Official Name: Republic of Korea, founded in 1948.

Official Language: Korean

Population: 45,000,000

Capital: Seoul (Population 10,000,000)

Currency: Won ₩

Land Area: 38,520 sq miles (99,392 sq km)

Ethnic Groups: Korean 99.9%; Others 0.1%

Religions: Protestant 19.7%; Nonreligious 48.9%; Buddhist 23.3%; Roman Catholic 6.7%; Confucian 0.4%

Major Physical Features: Highest point: Hallasan 6,398 ft (1,950 m); Longest river: Hangang 321 miles (514 km)

RUSSIA

N
W E
S

CHINA

PACIFIC OCEAN

AMNOKKANG

NORTH KOREA

PYONGYANG ■

DMZ (Demilitarized Zone)

EAST SEA (Sea of Japan)

Panmunjom ●

■ SEOUL

Inch'on ●

HAN-GANG (Han River)

WEST SEA (Yellow Sea)

SOUTH KOREA

● Kyongju

● Pusan

● Kwangju

Korea Strait

Chin-do

Cheju-do

▲ Halla-san

JAPAN

Scale
km 0   50   100   150
miles 0   50   100

MOUNTAIN BARRIERS AND LANDBRIDGES

Mountains are not far from any point along the Korean peninsula. The people revere them, position their houses by them, and climb them for recreation. Steep and difficult to traverse, the ranges long provided a barrier discouraging invasion from the north and southwest. In the past, neighboring countries repeatedly devastated Korea in their attempts to invade one another, or to claim the peninsula for themselves. Through the ages Korea has also been a cultural landbridge between China and Japan. Although each nation has its own culture, shared influences can be seen in architecture, dress, writing, religion, and government.

There were few roads in Korea until the twentieth century. Roadmaking was difficult in the rugged terrain and it was feared that roads would make it easier for invaders to travel along the landbridge. Goods were transported by boat to villages and carried on donkeys to mountain dwellers. Tracks were so narrow that it was hard for two carts to pass. Paved highways now make it easy to drive from one end of South Korea to the other in about four hours. In places the road suddenly widens to make an airstrip for emergency use.

▲ An ancient form of cross-country travel with wooden skis, using long poles for balance, was used before roads were built.

◄ The Kyongju Cherry Blossom Marathon is run on modern paved roads.

 ► A wooden-framed sliding door covered with *hanji*.

▲ Siberian tigers once roamed the mountains. To avoid their attacks, travelers gathered at an inn at the foot of a mountain and crossed the high passes as a group. Tigers are now almost extinct. Other animals found in Korea were brown bears, deer, and many birds, including the white crane.

▲ Pure mountain streams.

HANJI

(*Han* - Korea, *ji* - paper)
Korea's clear mountain streams, soil, and climate are perfect for production of *hanji*, a handmade paper. Famous for its beauty and strength, *hanji* is made from mulberry bark fibers and pure water. There is an old saying: "Canvas lasts for a hundred years: *hanji* lasts for a thousand years." Windows and doors of traditional houses were covered with just one layer of *hanji*. Thick, yellow paper floor coverings are still used. Those who have lived in such a house love the sound of the wind on the paper, and the way the sun and moon shine softly through it.

ISLANDS
About 3,000 rocky islands dot the south and east coasts. *Chindogae*, or loyal watchdogs, are bred on the island of Chin-do.

▼ The largest island is egg-shaped Cheju-do, a favorite holiday resort. In its center is Korea's highest mountain, Halla-san, an extinct volcano with underground lava tubes big enough to walk through for long distances. Cheju is known for its *haenyo*, women who dive for sea urchins, shellfish, and seaweed in the cold ocean waters. In spring Cheju is carpeted with brilliant yellow mustard flowers.

ARRIVAL OF THE FIRST KOREANS

Modern Koreans can trace their ancestors to a region of great mountains: the Altai, or Mountains of Gold, which stretch from icy Siberia to the Gobi Desert, and the Urals which separate northern Europe from Asia. Tribes migrated east across the vast grasslands, deserts, and mountains of northern Asia to the peninsula now called Korea. Clan communities established the first city-state, Choson, said to have been ruled from 2333 BC by the legendary Tangun, with his descendants reigning for a thousand years.

▲ Comb pottery decorated with sets of slanted lines was found both in Korea and Ural-Altaic regions, c. 3000 BC.

▲ The peninsula was named Choson, meaning "land of the morning calm," by the Chinese who could see the sun rise from its misty mountains.

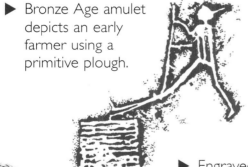

▶ Bronze Age amulet depicts an early farmer using a primitive plough.

▶ Engraved bells were made during Korea's bronze age and used by shamans in their dances.

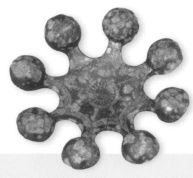

SPIRIT-SCARING FACES

These fearsome carvings were intended to ward off evil spirits. They were connected with primitive animist beliefs brought by settlers from northern Asia. Animism or shamanism is the belief that spirits live in all natural objects, in rocks, trees, rivers, and mountains, in the sea and in animals. Rituals were performed to these spirits by priests or shamans, who claimed supernatural powers. If someone was sick or had died, the shaman performed *kut*, chanting and dancing until he or she fell to the ground in a trance. The lasting influence of shamanism can be seen in contemporary Korean dance, and sometimes a business will have a *kut* performed in new premises.

EARLY KOREAN MIGRATION

The Korean language belongs to the Ural-Altaic family of languages which began in the region of the Ural and Altai mountains. It is quite different from Chinese. The red dots on the map show the direction of migration by early Korean settlers. Blue lines link other nations with the same Ural-Altaic language roots.

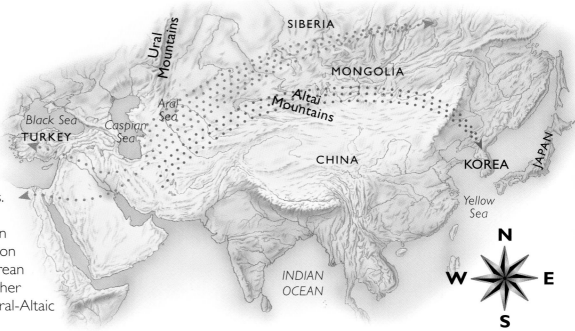

▲ The bases of early pit houses supported a cone-shaped straw or reed roof and had food storage holes and a fire pit in the center.

▼ Tying rice stalks for thatching. Many things were made from straw, including shoes, pots, and roofs.

▲ Rice-thatched houses were a later type of dwelling. They had earth walls and *ondol* underfloor heating.

▼ Later still came sturdy houses with timber pillars, clay walls, and tiled roofs.

BECOMING ONE NATION

The Korean tribes gradually developed over a period of a thousand years into one nation. By the first century AD, the tribes had grouped into three main kingdoms: Kogyuro, Paekche, and Shilla. As a colony of China for 400 years, their culture was patterned on the great Chinese dynasties of Han and Tang. The three kingdoms competed for power until, in AD 735, the Kingdom of Shilla overcame the others, removed Chinese control, and united Korea as one nation.

▲ Now a "museum without walls," Kyongju was once the capital of the Kingdom of Paekche. Festivals and parades retell the colorful history of the Three Kingdoms and the nation's beginning.

◄ Earrings and other precious artifacts have been found in the burial mounds of the Shilla kings ▼ at Kyongju.

◄ Shilla crown with many small pieces of jade and gold shaped like waves. When the king moved his head there was a ripple of chimes and light, symbolizing his godlike presence. Each piece of the king's clothing had some spiritual meaning.

▼ Skillfully crafted murals of hunters were painted 1,600 years ago in the tomb of a Koguryo king.

Peasants had no burial chambers or memorials. Their lives were considered of value only for serving the king and his court. When Shilla unified the nation, conditions improved for farmers. They were allotted land to grow rice, millet, and barley, and reservoirs were built for irrigation, using Chinese farming techniques such as the water wheel and flooding of paddy fields. Each farmer also had to raise cattle and horses and plant mulberry trees for silkworms. Part of their crop was returned to the government as tax.

BUDDHISM IN KOREA

Throughout Korea there are many pagodas and statues of the Buddha, an Indian prince who left his riches to meditate on the suffering of the world. By the time his ideas spread to Korea they were mixed with other religions, such as Hinduism and animism, and had become a religion with no god. Today monks live in temples where they work, meditate, and repeat rituals. They do this in the hope that, after going through countless rebirths in different bodies, they will eventually reach *Nirvana*, a perfect spiritual state free from all the evils of this world. Buddhist monks held important positions in the royal courts and Pulguksa, "Temple of the Buddha Land" (below), was built in the Shilla era.

KINGS AND POETS

▶ Poetry was enjoyed by scholarly courtiers and the best young men of Shilla, known as *Hwarangdo*, the "flower of youth" corps, were cultured soldiers trained in literature as well as war and community life. This clay drink vessel was shaped like a Shilla warrior.

▼ This stone-rimmed channel had a running stream used as a "timer" for a poetry game —a poem had to be written in the time it took a cup to float around the channel.

Hansi was a brief song-like poem written in Chinese (the only form of writing the Koreans had at that time). First used in Shilla in the ninth century, *hansi* poetry continued into the seventeenth century when poet Chong Chak wrote about the moment before dusk.

> At first I wondered if the figure
> on the distant sands was a white heron,
> but to the sound of piping on the wind,
> the vast expanse of sky and river faded into evening.

KORYO—KOREA

Korea's modern name comes from the Koryo dynasty, founded after rebels overthrew Shilla about 1,000 years ago. For 475 years Koryo kings tried unsuccessfully to reclaim vast territories once held in Manchuria. The court made Buddhism the state religion and granted great areas of land to its temples. However, when the monks and *yangban* (the upper class) became both greedy and powerful, the kingdom became weak and fell under the rebel "rule of the generals." Outside attacks came from Japanese pirates and from Mongols who, led by Genghis Khan and armed with iron weapons, were conquering the Asian continent. The Mongols overran Korea in AD 1231 and remained as overlords for the next century until the Koryo kingdom came to an end.

▲ *Tanchong*, the art of painting colored patterns on important wooden buildings.

A Mongol warrior.
▼

▲ The Korean court sought Buddha's protection from Mongol invasion, through the pious work of carving 81,258 woodblocks of the Buddhist scriptures. Called *Tripitaka Koreana*, they did not prevent invasion but are still stored in Heinsa temple.

▶ *Sandae* were masked plays in which the common people made fun of corrupt *yangban* and monks, just as today newspaper cartoons make fun of politicians. Plays mocked the sins of such characters as "The Pock Marked Monk" and "The Monk with Blinking Eyes." *Sandae* are still performed in Korean villages.

◄ Korea's famous celadon pottery has a beautiful milky glaze made from a secret formula. It was prized in China and Japan.

► A Confucian classroom by Kim Hong-do.

From the tenth century AD the Koryo court began to choose its officials by examination and guide its leaders and families by a strict set of Confucian rules. Schools taught boys academic subjects, while girls learned homemaking skills from their mothers. In the years following, education became highly valued and wise scholars were honored above others. Most Koreans would not call themselves Confucians now, but discipline and learning have influenced the Korean way of life.

CONFUCIANISM IN KOREA

Confucius was a philosopher born in China in 551 BC. His teaching became a pattern for society in China and other Asian countries. Of them all, Korea followed Confucianism most closely.

THE FIVE MOST IMPORTANT RULES
- Father and son—filial piety meant a son must always obey his father and care for him for life.
- Ruler and subject—people must be loyal to their country and king; the king must also listen to his advisors.
- Husband and wife—the wife must always obey her husband, stay home, bear sons, and serve her husband and children.
- Elder and younger—the younger person must always obey and honor those older.
- Friends—friends must be loyal to one another. This was the only equal relationship, although age was still honoured.

▲ The Confucian tradition of honoring ancestors is still observed. On occasions such as New Year many people dress in *hanbok*, the traditional Korean costume, and travel to visit grandparents. Children are taught to bow before their elders. After paying their repects at the graves of ancestors, families share a meal and play traditional games.

► A Confucian village elder.

CHOSON'S GOLDEN AGE

As the Mongols were ousted and the Ming Dynasty came to power in China, General Yi Song-gye took control in Korea and named the new kingdom Choson (after the ancient city-state of Choson). He built the capital, Han-yang, on the river where Seoul now stands. Choson's golden age, the high point of Korean civilization, occurred under King Sejong the Great, who loved learning and was particularly interested in the welfare of his people. He was concerned that only the educated *yangban* could write—and they wrote in Chinese which ordinary people could not read. The King's greatest achievement was the invention of a Korean alphabet called *hangul*, which enabled ordinary people to write their own language. For the first time they could communicate needs and feelings and express ideas in poetry and stories.

▲ A *taegum*, or flute, played by a court musician.

HANGUL, THE GREAT LETTERS

King Sejong's wisest scholars invented an alphabet scientifically based on the sounds of speech, and easy to learn and use.

- They *listened* carefully to the sounds made by people speaking.
- They *watched* how the parts of the mouth moved for each sound.
- They gave each sound a *written symbol*.
- Based on sounds, *hangul* is a phonetic system with 17 consonants and 11 vowels. (It differs from Chinese, in which 3,000 picture symbols must be memorized for basic use.)
- *Hangul* has been used since AD 1446 and remains Korea's unique national alphabet.

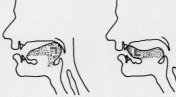

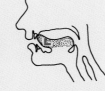

The sound "k" (as in "kick") is written imitating the shape of the tongue pulled back to the glottis.

The sound "n" (as in "nan") is written to show the tongue reaching up to the front gums.

▲ King Sejong the Great reigned from AD 1418 to 1450.

▼ Moveable metal type, first used before the thirteenth century, enabled a great output of books during the Choson dynasty.

▲ A self-chiming water clock.

Scientific inventions included a model of the solar system, a sundial, the pluviometer, a water clock, pulleys, and cranes. Books about farming and medicine, printed with moveable type, are still read today. Painting and literature reached high standards.

▲ A pluviometer or rain gauge.

◀ *Pyongjong*, a set of musical chimes or bells of differing thickness played with a horn mallet.

THE TURTLE BOAT NAVY

Today statues and festivals honor Admiral Yi Sun Shin who invented "turtle boats," the first armored battleships. Their oarsmen were protected below spiked decks of plaited iron, which looked like a turtle shell.

In a famous battle in AD 1592 the small turtle boats defeated the massive navy of the Japanese Emperor Hideyoshi, while on land, small bands of patriots fought the highly trained and heavily armed Japanese army.

Admiral Yi Sun Shin expressed the wish that, when he died, he might become a sea dragon and always guard Korea from invaders.

THE OLD ERA ENDS

▶ Westerners at the Korean Court. (Artist unknown.)

For 300 years after Japan's invasion in AD 1592, Choson kept its alliance with China but refused entry to other foreigners. As the last Asian country to begin trading with western nations, Korea was called the Hermit Kingdom. In the late 1600s reformers called for *Sirhak*, or "Practical Learning," to solve the problems of farmers and small merchants, and novels were written about the welfare of the people. Later, in the 1800s, when Roman Catholic priests came with trade ships from the west, their religion and culture were called *Sohak*, meaning "Western Learning." Both the religion and the traders were seen as a threat by the Confucian court and many *Sohak* followers were executed. In the unrest of the times, Korean nationalism emerged in a mixture of traditional religions known as *Tonghak*—"Eastern Learning." When flood, drought, and famine caused rebellion in the late 1800s, the peasants were rallied by the songs of *Tonghak*.

▲ *Cats and Sparrows*, painted on silk by Pyon Sang-byok, late seventeenth century.

▶ A brushmaker prepares fine bristle brushes for calligraphy and painting.

▶ With the rise of merchants in the seventeenth century, coins replaced the barter of goods.

The King's golden seal and its red ink mark or signature.

King Kojong is remembered for "coming down to the palace gate" to seek the opinion of the people. He and Queen Min reigned through the turmoil of the Choson Dynasty's last years. Steamships from Europe and America were bringing traders to East Asia, and Japan was also pressing for entry. From 1882, treaties unfavorable to Korea were signed. Japanese armies captured Manchuria and fought Russia on the Korean landbridge. Then in 1905, after secret meetings to gain the support of Western powers, Japan made Korea its protectorate, bringing Choson and the ancient era to an end.

▲ Queen Min was assassinated by Japanese officials in 1895. They are depicted here in *The Last Empress*, a modern drama.

Under Japanese occupation the young Crown Prince Yong-wang was taken hostage and forced to marry a Japanese princess. He lived in Japan for the rest of his life and never became king. He was the last heir to the Choson Dynasty, and Korea has had no king since then.

▼ Korea's Crown Prince Yong-wang with his wife and son, photographed when he returned to Korea on a visit in 1922.

▲ *Chogui* or Red Gown. This grand ceremonial gown with 132 pairs of pheasants embroidered in gold was sent to Japan for the Crown Princess.

WARS AND WORDS

After 1910, when Japan took control of Korea as its "protectorate," the Korean people were treated severely. They were often hungry while the crops they grew went to Japan and its armies. Hundreds of thousands of farmers were forced to move to Manchuria or Japan, and artists and craftspeople were sent to Japan. Roads, railways, and seaports were built for Japanese use. Korea remained under military control until Japan was defeated in 1945, at the end of World War II.

▲ The occupying Japanese took skilled potters and other Korean artisans to work in Japan.

▼ Proclamation of Korean Independence signed in 1919 by 33 patriots.

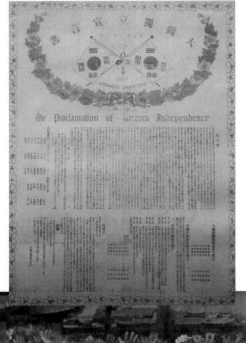

▲ From the time of Japan's occupation of Korea in 1905, guerrilla groups known as "righteous armies" gathered whatever weapons they could and resisted both in Korea and from overseas.

◄ This painting of the first Independence Day in March 1919 shows a reading of the Declaration of Independence. It was circulated secretly and crowds gathered all over Korea, shouting, *"Mansei! Mansei!"* ("May Korea live ten thousand years"). As punishment the military killed and wounded thousands. Foreign missionaries were the only people who could leave Korea to tell the world what was happening.

◀ Ryu Kwan-sun, who led an independence demonstration and later died from abuses while in prison.

CHRISTIANITY IN KOREA

Protestant missionaries, who arrived in the late nineteenth century, believed that all people were equal and they became leaders in the Korean struggle for freedom. They also set up hospitals and schools and helped women, for the first time, to take part in life outside their homes. The first school for girls opened in 1886 with one pupil only. The Protestant churches taught from their book, the Bible, that God loved all people, and that anyone who trusted in Jesus would be saved. This belief did not depend upon a class system and did not perform rituals to please or avoid spirits. Protestant churches continued after the occupation, to become one of South Korea's largest religions.

Reading and writing their own language was vital for Koreans during the colonial period, when Japanese language, culture, and history were officially taught in schools. Children were taught to think and feel as Japanese, not as Koreans. Even their names and religion were to be replaced. A group of teachers worked together to preserve the Korean language for future generations, while other patriots published *hangul* newspapers calling for freedom. The importance of these efforts to keep the national language alive was confirmed when many writers were arrested as "thought criminals" and died in prison.

▶ Present-day congregation leaving a Presbyterian church.

◀ A 1995 banner for Korea's celebrations 50 years after the end of occupation. Trade and peaceful relations are being resumed between Korea and Japan.

▲ The people of Seoul rejoiced at the news of Japan's surrender and Korea's liberation on 15 August 1945.

광복
50

THE BROKEN BRIDGE

▲
Left: North Korean Boys wearing the red scarf of Communist youth.

Right: South Korean boys in Scout uniform.

The children above are all Korean and some may be related, but they cannot play with or contact each other because their country is divided. They are separated by the DMZ (Demilitarized Zone)—a strip of land that cuts across the middle of the country. It is fenced with barbed wire and heavily guarded so that no one crosses. This divides the Korean people who had been one nation for more than a thousand years (since AD 735). At the end of World War II in 1945, Koreans celebrated their freedom, unaware that Allied countries had agreed that the USSR should share the work of restoring Korea after Japanese occupation. The USSR accepted Japanese surrender in the North; the United States in the South. But the United Nations' plan to establish an independent, united Korea was blocked by Communist North Korea. This confrontation led to civil war.

▲
Panmunjom, the gateway and official meeting place on the DMZ.

▶ Armed guards patrol the DMZ.

In 1950 North Korean armies invaded the South and the Korean War followed, devastating the land. After three years of bitter civil war, Korea was divided in 1953 by the Demilitarized Zone, stretching from coast to coast. Now there is an uneasy ceasefire between North and South, although the great hope of Koreans on both sides of the line is that they will be reunited in the future.

▲ Refugees from North Korea cross the shattered bridge over the Taedong River. Six million people fled south during the Korean War.

◀ North Korean army trucks move along paved roads that would allow them to enter South Korea quickly if there were a break in the DMZ. The North has dug several tunnels under the line.

▼ The United Nations Memorial Cemetery at Pusan honors foreign troops from 16 countries who died fighting alongside South Koreans.

▲ South Korean troops recapture Seoul in September 1950.

▲ South Korean tanks are always prepared for attack from the North. The cost of keeping an army always ready to defend is high. Other measures such as air-raid drills in Seoul are also costly and time-consuming. A United Nations peace-keeping force is stationed near the DMZ.

BUILDING A DEMOCRACY

In 1948 South Koreans chose a democratic form of government, but democracy did not come instantly to the new republic. The rule of a king had ended with Japanese occupation decades earlier, but it would take another 50 years to complete the change to an elected government with an opposition party. During the early years of the republic, military leaders kept control, pushing for fast economic growth, but there was little personal freedom. Since 1948 there have been six republics, nine constitutional changes, and many demonstrations by a people striving to reach their goal of a democracy. In December 1997, for the first time in Korean history, a candidate from an opposition party was freely elected president. North Korea became a Communist regime in 1948 and was ruled for many years by dictator Kim Il-sung.

▲ At the center of South Korea's flag is the *taeguk*, a Taoist symbol for the harmony of opposites.

◀ Kim Dae-jung, elected President of South Korea in 1997, said, "History will record that the Korean people decided to choose the opposition for the first time in 50 years."

DEMOCRACY IN SOUTH KOREA

The South Korean Constitution aims for a democratic government which gives responsibilities as well as privileges to both leaders and people. It states that all law-abiding citizens have the right to:

• leave and enter their homes as they wish
• meet with other people
• leave the country and return
• attend the church of their choice
• criticize government policies
• be treated equally by the law
• vote in free elections (both men and women)

These are momentous changes for Koreans after such a long struggle to achieve them.

▶ Workers on a footpath in Seoul watch a "talk to the people" television broadcast by the president.

▲ During the 1997–98 Asian financial crisis, Korea was unable to repay huge loans from the World Bank. To help their country, people of all ages stood in long lines to give their precious gold rings, ornaments, and keys to help repay the debt.

▼ Korea's unit of exchange is the *won* (₩).

South Korea, officially called the Republic of Korea, is like the United States of America, governed as a democratic republic with a president and three separate branches of power. The people of South Korea vote for their government leaders. Although their president is very powerful, the government has elected representatives and parties who can debate and discuss government policies.

▲ Parliament meets in the National Assembly building in Seoul, known as the Blue House.

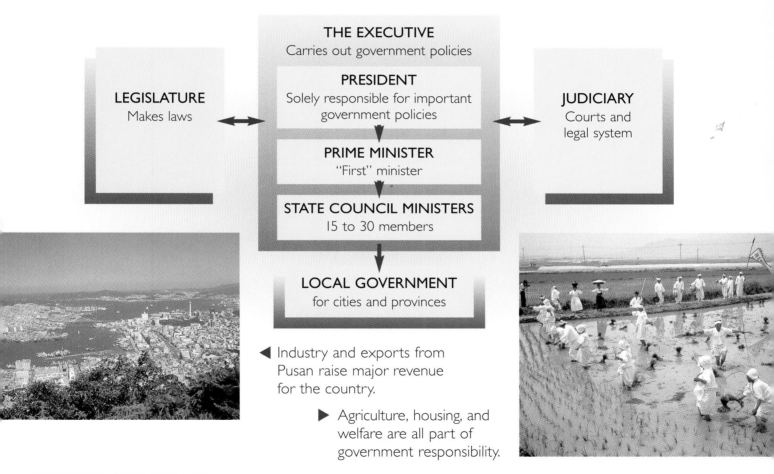

THE EXECUTIVE
Carries out government policies

PRESIDENT
Solely responsible for important government policies

PRIME MINISTER
"First" minister

STATE COUNCIL MINISTERS
15 to 30 members

LOCAL GOVERNMENT
for cities and provinces

LEGISLATURE
Makes laws

JUDICIARY
Courts and legal system

◀ Industry and exports from Pusan raise major revenue for the country.

▶ Agriculture, housing, and welfare are all part of government responsibility.

PROVERBS AND POLICY

The poetic language of Confucian officials is sometimes used by modern leaders to describe plans and policies. One proverb, "A river can only be clean when the upper reaches are clean," described two different clean-up policies—one was a practical clean-up of a polluted river, so that fish returned and water sports could be enjoyed; the other was a promise to clean up corruption in the "upper reaches" of government.

Former President Kim Young-sam, a long-time freedom-fighter, used a flower to define freedom with responsibility. He said, "…the true meaning of freedom is to *plant* a flower in the park rather than to *pick* a flower from the park."

SOUTH KOREA AND THE WORLD

South Korea has the proud record of never having invaded another country. Having allied itself with democratic nations, South Korea has moved from its former economy based on local villages and self-sufficiency, into wide contact with other countries of the world, both in trade and in political, cultural, and social interchange and cooperation. South Korea contributes much to others and welcomes new ideas.

▲ *Taekwondo,* which originated in Korea, is physical exercise and martial art designed to develop mind and body. *Taekwondo* was an official sport in the Year 2000 Olympics in Sydney.

▼ A sericulture research center offers a training program in silkworm farming. Women from Iran learn methods for growing improved silkworms and mulberry leaves, and techniques of reeling and processing silk.

▶ Former President Kim Young-sam escorted by a Canadian Mounted Policeman in Vancouver, where he attended a summit meeting of APEC (Asia-Pacific Ecomomic Cooperation) in 1997 during the Asian financial crisis.

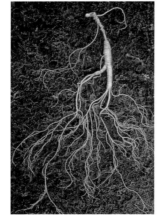

▲ The root of Korean ginseng is valued for medicinal uses. It is taken by many athletes worldwide to improve stamina.

▼ A bird sanctuary near Pusan provides a safe stopover habitat for migratory geese.

▲ Korean families living in other countries make opportunities to meet and learn traditional music and dances. *Hanbok*, the national costume, is often worn on festive occasions.

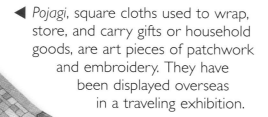

◄ *Pojagi*, square cloths used to wrap, store, and carry gifts or household goods, are art pieces of patchwork and embroidery. They have been displayed overseas in a traveling exhibition.

▲ Staged on Broadway, New York, the Korean musical *The Last Empress* dramatized Queen Min's final days.

◄ Korea's Chunchon International Mime Festival has attracted foreign participants since 1994, including groups from Japan, Israel, Poland, and the United States.

◄ Taking part in an international aid program, this Korean doctor provides medical attention in Nepal.

▼ Popular sports include bicycle racing, athletics, soccer, and baseball.

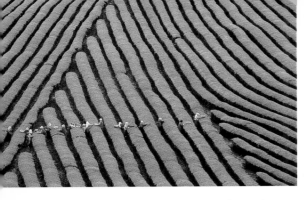

FOOD FROM SUN, SOIL, AND SEA

South Korea has one of the world's highest rice yields and is self-sufficient in food grains, although only 30 percent of its land is arable. Farmers, using modern machinery and scientific methods, can grow two crops of rice and barley each summer. Rice fields are terraced as they have been for centuries. A rural education movement has been active in teaching modern farming methods, and helping village communities organize cooperative projects, such as installation of electricity and water supplies.

▲ Tea-pickers move along plantation rows filling baskets with leaves.

▼ Although modern farm equipment is used to harvest summer crops, some farmers continue to wear the cool white cotton clothes of Korean tradition.

◀ Pigs are moved to new pens in a system of scientific intensive farming, carried out in hygienic conditions. Several pig farmers formed a company that grows, prepares, and markets pork of the highest quality.

Vegetables thrive, and temperate climate fruits include peaches, apples, pears, persimmons, and strawberries. Fish, plentiful in the sea around the peninsula, provide a large part of the Korean diet and exports. The West Sea, shallow because of the continental shelf, is a fertile environment for shellfish and seaweed. Deep seas to the east and south are excellent fishing grounds, and oceangoing fishing fleets travel long distances. However, they are restricted by the zones that protect the fishing grounds of other nations. There are also inland fish farms.

▲ Persimmons and other summer fruits are preserved by sun-drying.

▼ A handful of squid, caught in various sizes and cooked in many ways, is popular in the fish markets.

▲ Sun-drying fish—
◀ one of the oldest and best methods of preserving food —reduces water content so that no bacteria grows in the food and the flavor is retained.

MIRACLE OF THE HAN

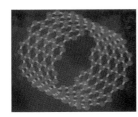

▲
Nanotubes, a new semiconductor, said to be 100 times stronger than steel.

The economic progress of South Korea following the Korean War was so amazing that it has been called the miracle of the Han. Using loans from international banks, South Korea has built a modern technology, making it a world leader in many industries. Recovering from the destruction of war, it also achieved a high standard of living, with comfortable healthy dwellings, schools, and leisure facilities. Small businesses began this manufacturing miracle by making little things like hairclips, T-shirts, and sandals. Because people were willing to work long hours for low wages, the country was able to acquire more efficient equipment to enable increase in industries. In the late 1990s a massive slump in Asian economies has caused Korea severe financial problems, making it necessary to cut back once again and reorganize production.

◀ Footwear manufacture began during the war period using waste rubber. Now, Korea is a leading supplier of upscale sport shoes.

▲ Decorative glass, plate glass, and armored glass are all manufactured and exported.

▶ Researchers working on sophisticated electronic equipment sleep on the *ondol* floor when exhausted. They have won world recognition and awards in the field of high-frequency wireless communications.

Steel production has grown rapidly since 1980. It is sold worldwide along with industrial and electronic equipment, cars, petrochemicals, cement, chemicals, processed food, textiles, and footwear. Business leaders encourage greater effort by calling Korea "the land of can-do." Family businesses such as Samsung and Hyundai, called *chaebols*, have become giant companies employing thousands of workers in Korea and across the world. Korea has few natural resources so it imports materials to manufacture export goods. As in all industrial countries, the need to decrease pollution is urgent.

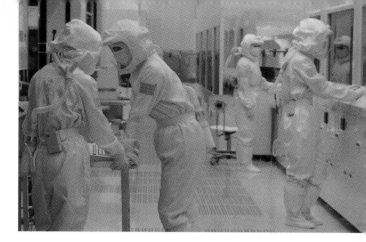

▲ Wearing dust-free clothing, workers produce memory chips the size of a thumbnail, able to store data equal to 2,000 newspapers.

▼ South Korean shipyards have built some of the world's largest vessels, and have been noted for their speed and efficiency.

▲ Textiles, one of the earliest industries, now includes new synthetic fibers and fashion garments.

▼ The petrochemical industry refines imported crude oil to produce resins and raw materials for synthetic fibers.

▲ Car manufacturers are working to develop fuel-efficient cars to add to their exports.

SEOUL CITY

Seoul (pronounced "sole") is the capital of South Korea. It is also its largest city, with more than ten million people. Travelers flying in to land at Kimpo Airport can see the city spread across a valley encircled by mountains.

Skyscrapers rise along the Han-gang, which flows through the city center. The name Seoul means "capital." Here and there among the glass and steel buildings of the modern city can be seen some of the old palaces and temples of the Kingdom of Choson, built 600 years ago in this valley. Most of the old city was destroyed during the Korean War, but it rose from the ashes and has grown rapidly to become the lively political, cultural, educational, and economic center of South Korea.

▲ Children wearing *hanbok*, the traditional dress of Seoul's early period, worn today for festive occasions.

▲ Theme parks and expositions offer Disneyland-style fun in Seoul. This is a Caribbean water ride.

◄ A traditional symbol representing the harmony of humanity, earth, and heaven.

▲ The Olympic Peace Gate is shaped like a phoenix, a mythical bird said to burn itself on its funeral pyre and rise from the ashes as a new young bird. It is a symbol of modern Seoul, rebuilt from the rubble of war.

◄ Cars swirl around the old South Gate, once an entrance through the walls of the old city of Choson. The phoenix is painted under the arch of the main city gate, through which only the king could enter.

▼ An early map of Seoul shows the city walls and present-day gate.

For many people in the world, their introduction to Korea was the spectacular opening ceremony of the 1988 Olympic Games in Seoul. The hospitable Korean people welcomed the nations of the world into their city and their homes. Today visitors can enjoy modern theme parks or very old temples, see artisans working, or take a river ferry or a fast train into the country—it is not far to the mountains and smaller cities such as Kyongju. Museums, galleries, expositions, and festivals are popular, since most families live in apartments and go out for recreation.

▲ A ferry ride is a popular outing.

▲ Subways are made attractive—this one has an art exhibition; others have fountains to clean the air.

PEOPLE IN A CHANGING SOCIETY

It is a huge task to change the way of life of a whole country. The South Korean economy has been rebuilt in the last 40 years. Before this change most of the people lived in rural villages, grew their own food, and made almost everything they needed, or traded for it in the village market. Now most people live in cities and trade is carried out through large businesses at home and overseas. So a person who once worked in a rice field may now be a shipbuilder, factory worker, or scientist. There are difficulties—some people have no work, and all are affected by change in the world economy. However, the studious, hard-working Koreans have been good at modernizing and adapting to change.

1963
37% live in cities

63% live in the country

POPULATION CHANGES 1963 to 1995

In the Republic of Korea (South Korea) the population almost doubled from 25 million in 1963 to 45.2 million in 1995.

1995
12.5% live in the country

87.5% live in cities

Compare the pie charts, which show the change from country to city living:

In 1963:
15.75 million lived in the country.
9.25 million lived in cities.

By 1995:
5.65 million lived in the country.
39.55 million lived in cities.

HOUSING CHANGES

◀ An old-style rural house with a mountain behind and water in front, which was thought to bring luck. Once, grandparents, married sons, and their families all lived in one house.

▶ With so many people moving into the city, housing became a problem. The government has built huge apartment blocks where most married couples have a unit to themselves.

City-dwellers use the most up-to-date technology and wear western dress, while in rural villages, families enjoy a mixture of old and new lifestyles. Parents educate their children to succeed in a modern western-style culture. Older people remember the struggle of rebuilding Korea after occupation and war, and some worry that Korean culture is being lost; they wish to keep such values as attention to studies, courtesy to elders, the enjoyment of simple pleasures, and the ability to endure and overcome hardship.

▲ Old religions are often mixed with new. Animist prayers to a "tree-spirit" take place next to a Buddhist pagoda.

▲ The International Trade Building in Seoul is the center of buying and selling with other countries. Korea now finds it difficult to repay large overseas loans.

▲ In self-supporting villages, housewives select fresh locally grown vegetables and grains.

◀ Before clothes manufacturing was industrialized, fabric was hand-spun and woven at home from natural fibers such as cotton or silk.

KAH JOK—THE FAMILY

Family (*kah jok*) is at the center of Korean life. Traditionally, family life has been organized in the Confucian way—one person is head of the house, and all others have their own position in the family. The parents' most important duty is to educate their children, and children are expected to bring honor to the family name by studying to achieve success at school and in later life. The father is the "outside person"—he must provide income for his wife and children as well as his parents. He spends long days at his work and often meets with business associates or friends afterwards, so he spends little time with his family or on household matters. The mother is the "inside person" who cares for the needs of her children and takes responsibility for the home. Often the husband gives all his salary to his wife, who manages the house and gives him an allowance.

▲ Small family groups travel the country performing acrobatics and folk dances.

▲ Ice-sledding is a popular winter activity for children throughout South Korea.

▲ Father and younger children enjoy a game of *paduk* at home while mother and an older daughter prepare food. *Paduk* competitions are held across Korea; playing skills are taught by one generation to the next.

NAMES

Names are important and are carefully chosen.
- Many people share the same family name. Almost half of all South Koreans are named either Kim, Lee, or Park. Other names often used are An, Chung, Choe, Chang, Han, Kang, Yi, Yu—so how do Koreans know which person is being named?
- There are multitudes of different given names which are used with the family name.
- The title and family name are placed first with given names second; for example: Mr. Kim Kun-hee, Ms. Park Young-mee.

▶ In a traditional funeral, a procession with a white bier honoring the dead person made its way to the burial site with much ceremony. This type of funeral is rare today.

▲ At a traditional marriage ceremony the newlywed couple sit at a table loaded with delicacies.

The family genealogy (record of members of a family) is kept carefully. The family is traced through the male members. Girls are recognized as valued members of the family, but because they will have the name of the man they marry, they are not included in the family line.

HOW FAMILIES ARE ORGANIZED

Halabuji receives honor as the head of the family. When grandfather dies, his eldest son becomes head of the family and receives honor and responsibility.

Halmoni obeys Halabuji and receives honor as his wife.

Ah deul takes care of his parents and wife and children, and will inherit the role of head of family.

Boo in obeys Ah deul and Halabuji.

The eldest male in the family is expected to be wise and fair in guiding his family. Younger family members are expected to obey him absolutely.

The correct name to call a person is a complicated matter, depending on who is older and who is speaking. The words for "brother" or "sister" are different according to whether the speaker is older or younger. If a boy speaks of his brother he uses a different word than a girl speaking of her brother.

A FAMILY TREE

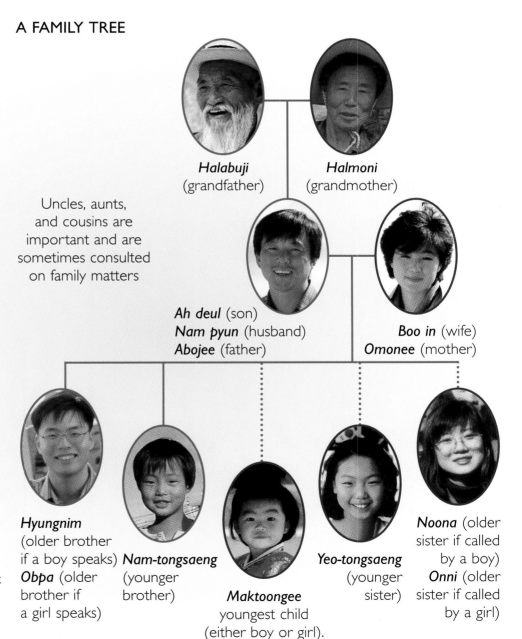

Uncles, aunts, and cousins are important and are sometimes consulted on family matters

Halabuji (grandfather)

Halmoni (grandmother)

Ah deul (son)
Nam pyun (husband)
Abojee (father)

Boo in (wife)
Omonee (mother)

Hyungnim (older brother if a boy speaks)
Obpa (older brother if a girl speaks)

Nam-tongsaeng (younger brother)

Maktoongee youngest child (either boy or girl).

Yeo-tongsaeng (younger sister)

Noona (older sister if called by a boy)
Onni (older sister if called by a girl)

Kimchi

FOOD FOR ALL OCCASIONS

Korean food has a variety of dishes for all occasions. Rice is the basic food eaten at every meal with *kimchi* and other spicy side dishes. Fish, chicken, beef, and pork are combined with rice and many vegetables. Some meals, such as those celebrating a marriage, are formal and ceremonial. Feasts are prepared for special birthdays and holidays such as New Year. Many people also offer food in religious rituals such as Buddha's birthday or in honor of ancestors. For people wanting to eat in a hurry there are street vendors selling tasty hot snacks or packaged food.

▲ *Kuljolpan* is served with pancakes and a choice of fillings.

▼ A medicine chest has small drawers for storage of dried herbs and other natural remedies such as plants or animal horns or innards.

▲ The *tol*, a feast held on a child's first birthday, is an important event. Gifts of money and gold rings from family and friends are kept for the child's future needs, such as education or marriage.

◀ Rituals in honor of ancestors include offerings of food.

▲ *Hanjongshik*, a full Korean meal. People sit on cushions on the floor at a low table. Rice and soup are placed at each place, with hot dishes on the right and cold on the left.

▶ In autumn, Korea's favorite dish, *kimchi*, is made with pickled cabbage and other vegetables mixed and fermented with spices and chili.

TABLE MANNERS

- Children do not begin eating until the adults pick up their spoons.
- Do not leave the table until the elders have finished eating.
- It used to be bad manners to talk while eating, but now many people chat.
- Silence is still considered a sign of enjoyment of the meal.
- Eat the foods in any order you like.
- A spoon is used for rice and soup, chopsticks for side dishes.
- Slurping is sometimes heard, but never blow your nose at the table (in Korea or anywhere else!).

◀ Coke and apples at the bus stop.

▼ Hot takeaway food from a roadside stall.

▶ Tasting soy sauce, which is the basis for *kimchi* and many other Korean dishes.

▲ Girls learning to use machine equipment at a technical college. There are also vocational colleges that prepare young people for work in service occupations such as tourism, transport, food shops, theme parks, health, and sports.

EDUCATION

With one of the highest literacy rates in the world, South Korea considers well-educated people a precious resource. The most important duties of children are to respect their parents and to carry out their school work thoroughly. They attend school five and a half days each week and, as they are expected to work so hard at school, children do not usually have home chores. Mothers are therefore busy with housework and supervising the children's activities. With both young people and parents working long hours, there is little time for leisure, but great enthusiasm for sporting and cultural activities such as music.

▶ Working after school on his computer, this senior student created a software program to handle different forms of data. After completing his studies, he launched his own company to market it.

A TYPICAL DAY FOR AN ELEVEN-YEAR-OLD

- **7 am**: Get up and dress. Mother packs two lunch boxes for each child—one for after school.
- **8.30 am**: School assembly. The principal makes announcements and the children thank the principal. Classrooms will have between 50 and 70 students who sit at desks facing front, or in small groups.
- There are eight main subjects in primary school: moral education, Korean language, social studies, arithmetic, science, physical education, music, and fine arts.
- **3 pm**: After school the children help clean their school buildings. Many then attend private classes such as art, music, or English language.
- **8.30 pm**: Home, with another two or three hours of homework.
- **10 or 11 pm**: Bed.

◀ The symbol of Seoul National University forms its main gate.

At school I will learn Korean and English, and another foreign language such as Japanese, Chinese, German, or French.

Girls and boys must complete six years of primary school. From age 12 to 14 years they attend middle school, and from 15 to 17 years, high school. Students who want an academic career such as law, arts, or science, must maintain a high standard during school and pass a national examination to enter one of the 164 universities. Colleges offer long or short courses of various types—agriculture, technical, trade, commercial, marine, arts, or comprehensive—for young people and adults.

▲ Between classes these primary school students practice the *komungo*, a classical instrument.

◀ Technical colleges provide laboratories where students can perform experiments.

▲ Giant ants in an outdoor science display, one of the many places to learn and have fun in museums of science, history, and arts and crafts, such as a Paper Museum.

◀ Children can go to preschool until they begin school at six years of age.

▲ Tourist brochures welcome visitors to Korea with two little characters, a boy, Chorong-ee, and a girl, Saekdong-ee. They carry a lantern (*chongsa chorong*) traditionally used to guide guests from the gate to the house.

▼ Try to speak Korean—you will find people friendly and helpful.

VISITING KOREA

Visitors are welcomed and well cared for in Korea, and their mistakes will be kindly excused. For their part, visitors can show courtesy by learning the customs of the country. Korean people will be pleased when you try to speak their language—it is one of the easiest in the world. Introductions are a vital part of Korean life, and follow the pattern of younger to older, less important to the more important person. Koreans' attitude to people they have been introduced to is very different from their attitude to strangers. Seeing South Korea means going to the mountains, watching colorful folk dances, exploring hands-on science exhibits, and perhaps staying in a *minbak*, a family home where you can experience traditional Korean living.

▲ Many museums and galleries present aspects of Korean culture, such as this demonstration of traditional printing techniques.

◀ The snow season lasts about three months. Winter sports are popular with tourists and Koreans alike.

◀ *Yogwan* are budget-priced inns found in cities and towns. Often located next door to a *yogwan* is a *mogyoktang*, where travelers and locals can relax in tiled pools of steaming hot water. Before entering the pool, soap and scrub yourself clean, then after a relaxing soak, take a cold shower and very hot sauna.

Say it in KOREAN!
Thank you – *Kam-sa hamni-da*
How are you? – *Anyong haseyo*
Goodbye – *Anyonghi kasipsiyo*

◀ Because Koreans sit, eat, and sleep on the floor, you must remove your shoes before entering a house or, as here, a temple.

▼ With long hat-ribbons whirling, the farmers' dance is full of color, action, and noise.

KOREAN COURTESY

Try to understand how Korean people think and act.
- *Kibun* is very important to Koreans. It is about treating people so as not to upset their feelings, not to embarrass or hurt their dignity.
- *Nunchi* is about judging how others feel. This is not easy since Koreans have been taught to hide their feelings and do not express ideas directly.
- Koreans smile when they are embarrassed and stare when they are angry. They tend to put off making a decision, and they always think about the status of a person and treat each accordingly.

▼ To reach the summit of Taedunsan requires steady nerves—you must walk across this steel rope bridge stretched precariously between two craggy pinnacles.

INDEX

How to use the Index
Words in standard type are specific references.
Words in **bold** type are general subject references;
the word itself may not appear on each page listed.

PICTURE CREDITS

Abbreviations: r = right, l = left,
t = top, c = center, b = below

**Korean National Tourist
Organization**
Cover, Title; **8** tl, bl, tr; **10** bl, c, r;
11 cl, bl, c; **12** bl, tr; **13** bl, cr, br;
14 tl; **15** tl, br; **16** tl, tr, br; **17** tl, bl;
18 tl; **19** bl, c; **20** bc, tr; **23** cr; **24** tr;
27 l, tr, cr, br; **28** tl, c, br; **29** br;
30 tl, b; **31** tr; **33** bl, cr; **34** tl, bl, tr, br;
35 cr; **36** tr, br; **37** tl, bl, c, tr, br;
38 tl, br; **39** *Halabuji*; *Yeo-tongsaeng*;
40 tl, cl, cr, bc; **41** tl, c, br; **42** b;
44 tl, cl, c, bl, r; **45** tr, b.

***Seoul* Magazine**
11 r; **13** cl; **18** br; **21** bl, tc, tr, br;
23 br; **26** cl, c, tr; **28** bl, tr; **29** bl, tr, cr;
30 tr; **32** tl, bl, br; **33** tr, br; **35** tr, br;
38 tr; **39** *Halmoni, Hyungnim, Noona*;
42 tl, r; **43** cl, tr, cr.

Mike Langford
Contents; Introduction; **8** br; **10** tl, cl;
14 b; **15** tr; **17** br; **24** tl; **25** c, br; **30** cl;
31 cl, bl, br; **34** c; **35** tl; **36** tl, bl; **38** cl;
39 tl, *Ah deul, Boo in, Nam-tongsaeng,
Maktoongee*; **41** bl, bc; **43** tl, bl; **45** tl.

**Consulate-General of
the Republic of Korea**
11 tl; **12** tl, br; **14** cl, c, cr; **15** c;
17 tr; **19** tl, tr, br; **20** tl; **22** tl, bl, c, tr;
23 tl, bl; **24** bl, br; **25** tl, bl, tr; **26** tl.

**Korean Overseas
Information Service**
15 bl; **18** tc, bc, tr; **20** br;
Korea Trading Post **Magazine**
32 c; **33** cl.

Chosun Gallery, Sydney
40 bl.

Valerie Hill
29 tl.

Peter Barker
12 c; **16** cl (artwork).

Ray Sim
9 map; **13** map.

Every effort has been
made to consult all
relevant people and
organizations. Any
omissions or errors
are unintentional
and should be
reported to Vineyard
Freepress Pty Ltd.